NAVIGATE THE
PATH TO AUTHORSHIP©

Elsa Kurt

Copyright ©Elsa Kurt
ISBN: 978-1-7346458-2-8

All rights reserved. No part of this publication may be reproduced, distributed, or transmitted in any form or by any means, including photocopying, recording, or other electronic or mechanical methods, without the prior written permission of the publisher, except in the case of brief quotations embodied in critical reviews and certain other noncommercial uses permitted by copyright law. For permission requests, write to the publisher, addressed "Attention: Permissions Coordinator," at the address below.

authorelsakurt@gmail.com
www.elsakurt.com

Ordering Information:
Quantity sales. Special discounts are available on quantity purchases by corporations, associations, and others. For details, contact the publisher at the address above.
Orders by U.S. trade bookstores and wholesalers. Please contact authorelsakurt@gmail.com or visit www.elsakurt.com.

Printed in the United States of America

This is a work of fiction. Names, characters, businesses, places, events, locales, and incidents are either the products of the author's imagination or used in a fictitious manner. Any resemblance to actual persons, living or dead, or actual events is purely coincidental.

Contents

FOREWORD 1

1 Introduction 2

2 The Nutshell 5

3 Goal Setting 7

4 What Kind of Writer Are You? 8

5 Write. 9

6 Roadblocks to Writing 11

7 Elements of A Story 15

8 Inside the Outline 18

9 Dust, Vacuum, & Polish (AKA: Editing) 20

10 To Self-Publish 24

11 The Nutshell 30

12 To Traditionally Publish 32

13 The Nutshell 38

14 Next Steps 39

15 Newsletters 44

16 Putting Yourself Out There 46

17 The Nutshell 49

18 Now What? 50

19 The Nutshell 55

20 Navigating the Book Selling Circuit 56

21 Congratulations 58

22 Paid Promoting 60

23 The Nutshell 63

24 Resources 64

25 Glossary of Common Terms 70

26 Final Words 74

FOREWORD

I am a self- and traditionally published author of twelve novels, two writer's guidebooks, several children's books, and short stories. I've had work selected for publication by Chicken Soup for the Soul, Tales2Inspire, as well as been quoted in Authors Should Speak by Dan Blanchard.

I've attended more than a hundred author events, and spoken before numerous groups, as well as been interviewed in print, Youtube channel shows, television, radio, and podcasts.

Throughout 2018, 2019, and present, I've presented both my You Wrote It, Now What and my Path to Authorship programs to various groups, as well as taught an adult enrichment program for new and aspiring writers.

In 2019, I began my Path to Authorship one on one mentoring program & have successfully coached several writer's to authorship. I offer: Consulting (one on one or group) Coaching & Self-Publishing Assistance.

Elsa Kurt Email: authorelsakurt@gmail.com
Social: @authorelsakurt Social @pathtoauthorship
Website: elsakurt.com

1 Introduction

If you're at all like me, when you want information, you want it now. You don't want to sift through, or scroll down, or wait for the goods. Great news. This introduction here? This is the one and only bit of fluff in the whole book. I had to do it, because every book must set the tone for the *rest* of the book.

It also gives the author a chance to talk about themselves gratuitously. We give you the "mission statement" of the forthcoming pages, tell you why it was so important to the author to write the book, and oh, some "about me," blah, blah, blah. You know, the boring stuff. Ready? So, one of the things people question when they pick up a book from a so-called (or perceived) expert, is: what's their credentials? Also known as Who Do They Think They Are? Therefore, I'll tell you who and what I am. But first, who and what I am not. I am not a New York Times best-selling author. Yet. I am not independently wealthy of the royalties of the sales of my books. I'm not internationally known (at least, I don't think I am). And if you sang Rob Base lyrics after reading that part, we should be friends. Now, here is what I am. I am you. Or at some point, I was you. I was a person dreaming about writing and then publishing a book. And so, I did. And that I did it again, and again, and again… I did it about twenty times, to be exact. That's as of the time of publishing this book. During each of those times, I learned what not to do, and I also learned what to do in order to get my books out into the universe.

I began with a self-published children's book and followed it with a few more. They were good, but not great. I learned more things, improved them, re-released them. Someday, when I'm less involved in other projects, I'll return to them with the knowledge I've gained, and improve them again. Maybe. Or, maybe I'll just let them be what they are and write new books.

When the compulsion to write didn't wane after those books, I tackled the young adult novel I'd been dreaming of for countless years. I wrote it over the course of a year, self-published it, and waited for something magical to happen. Nothing did. Lesson one: you must make magical things happen through work and perseverance.

I can tell you, with due embarrassment, that the book was not very good. More precisely, the story was good, the writing… eh, not so much. I still had a lot to learn. So, I educated myself through the school of hard knocks, internet, and… reading books. By the way, no one told me it, er, sucked. I reread it with a more objective and critical eye a couple years later. I pulled it from distribution and sales, retooled it, and will eventually re-release it. Since those days, I've written and published—both traditionally and self-published—about fifteen novels, three novellas, eight children's books, and several upcoming books. My work has appeared in the beloved series, [Chicken Soup for the Soul](), as well as [Tales2Inspire](), and [Authors Should Speak](). I've coached aspiring authors to authorship, spoken before hundreds, taught a writer's course, and created an online community for new and aspiring writers. I've been interviewed for television, podcasts, YouTube channels, and print. Humblebrag over.

Along my writing journey, I've encountered so many people who've expressed a desire to publish their stories but lacked in the know-how or courage. This resonated and touched me because I was once where they are. I was terrified at the idea of allowed others to read and then judge my work. I was baffled by the process. Those factors together held me back for years. And then they didn't. The only thing that has equaled the exhilaration of publishing book, is the realization that I've helped someone else pursue their dream and goal. The first time this happened—I'd been asked to speak on a panel of authors about navigating the convention circuit—I felt a rush of excitement at the looks on some of the attendees faces when I spoke about my writing journey. What I was saying—little old me—impacted and affected them. They thanked *me* for helping *them*.

From then on, it's been my passion to not only write, but to help my fellow writers navigate their path to authorship. And there, my friends, is my *Why*. I tried to condense it as much as reasonable, but let's be honest. You've probably skipped right over the introduction and that's okay. I usually do, too.

2 The Nutshell

Right here (okay, below here) is the outline of your publishing plan. Each chapter after will delve into the phases of your plan.

- **Write**.
- Create a writing routine
- Set a publishing goal/timeline
- Understanding word count & word count goals
- Write your manuscript

- **Edit**
- Self-edit
- Beta/Proofreaders
- Editor
- Pre-Publishing

- Self-Publishing- pros and cons
- Traditional Publishing – pros and cons
- Building your platform
- Using platform for pre-promotion
- Designing marketing materials

- **Promote**

- Website
- Social media
- Bookstores
- Events

3 Goal Setting

Get Motivated

Setting your writing goals helps you solidify and visualize your intentions. Have these goals written out and placed somewhere visible—like beside your laptop or on your mirror—to keep you on task.

Stay On Task

- MY DAILY (OR WEEKLY) WORD COUNT GOAL IS_____
- MY FIRST DRAFT COMPLETION DATE WILL BE_____
- MY FINAL DRAFT COMPLETION DATE IS_____
- MY PUBLISHING GOAL IS _____

Plan of Action

As you progress in your manuscript, and while keeping your publishing goal in mind, you'll want a plan of action for the other tasks in your path to authorship journey.

For Example

- BEGIN FIRST ROUND EDITS ON_____
- BEGIN SECOND ROUND EDITS ON _____
- (REPEAT AS NECESSARY)
- BETA/PROOFREADERS MUST FINISH BY_____

4 What Kind of Writer Are You?

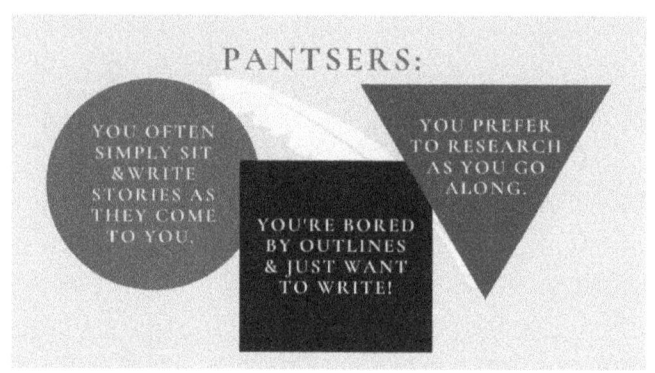

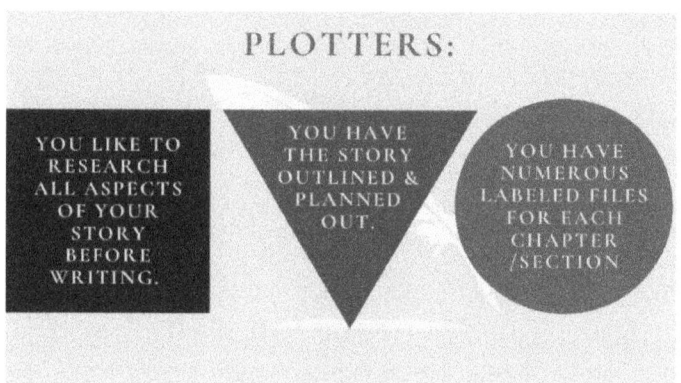

5 Write.

When an established author tells you that the first step in getting a book published is to write the book, they're not being snarky. Okay, maybe they're being a little bit snarky. But the truth is, is that it is that simple. You have to sit down and write the book. Procrastinating, doubting, questioning, and thinking about writing a book will not get a book written. Dwelling on how to get it published will not get your book written.

Fantasizing about New York Times best-selling author status will not get a book written. Planting your ass in a chair and writing the book; that's what will get a book written.

I'm not trying to be facetious, nor do I think you are obtuse. You're doing exactly what people—including myself—tend to do. We put off things that are hard. We say things like, "When life slows down a little, then I'll have time to write." Well, guess what, buttercup? It ain't slowing down. Make time. You have to make time to write. If you want to accomplish this vague but insistent goal, that is. I'll go out on a limb here and say that, if this book or any one like it is in your possession, this is a serious goal of yours. That means you won't mind if I give you some tough love. Here it is: Stop talking about writing a book and write the damn book.

For some of you, that might mean dusting off that old manuscript you've been pecking at on and off for years. That's okay. Better than okay, actually. You've got a base, a beginning.

For others, that means sitting down in front of a blank screen (or notebook) with sweaty palms and a conflicting sense of fluttery anticipation and trepidation. I can't speak for you, but the promise of a blank page, waiting for words to fill it? Swoon.

Still for some, it's somewhere in the hazy in between. You've several starts of stories. A bunch—no, a ton—of ideas for stories… but where to begin? I'll bet you see a story in just about everything. The old man crossing the street sparks a story in your mind. The couple arguing quietly at the next table. The mist over a lake. Stories, stories, everywhere stories.

6 Roadblocks to Writing

The one thing all the above "types" have in common is, you're stuck. So, let me figuratively hold your hand and get you through the phases. The following chapters will take you through the steps of bringing your story from concept to publishing, and on to marketing.

Let's address the most common roadblocks to writing.

I. **Roadblock Number One** <u>Time</u>. Listen, we are busy as heck, I know. Work, kids, spouses/partners, commitments & obligations, housework… the list is endless. And when we do find time? We're exhausted. And yet, I still say, MAKE time. Not find time, make time. It's there tucked in between this and that. Even if it's twenty minutes, it counts.

II. **Roadblock Number Two** <u>Energy</u>. It goes hand in hand with time. One might think, "Why do I need energy to sit and type (or write)?" The simple answer is your brain needs to be firing on all cylinders to write anything of merit. If you're feeling meh when it's time to write, take a few minutes to do something physical/mildly exertive or stimulating. (I walk on the treadmill for ten minutes.) Eat brain food (oh, hell, have some chocolate!). Psych yourself up the hour before writing by listening to anything that motivates you- music, podcast, Tony Robbins, whatever does the job.

III. **Roadblock Number Three** <u>Procrastination</u>. For as much as I deeply love writing, I am guilty of procrastinating... often. Maybe it's because I know that once I sit down behind the computer, it'll be hours before I get up again. Or maybe it's just my ADD. Whatever the case, I stall and allow myself to get distracted by every little thing. So, my solution is TIMERS! Yep, I set the timer. 30 minutes to run around, or mindlessly scroll Facebook, or stare at the wall. It works about 90% of the time.

V. **Roadblock Number Four** <u>Inspiration</u>. You know how it is. Sometimes (usually when driving, sleeping, or in the shower) inspiration hits and the ideas are like endless waterfalls that you can't get onto paper or screen fast enough. And then there are the times when you can't get past the word "The." You can handle this effectively in two very different ways. 1) Walk away & relax, it'll come back to you. Panicking will only chase the idea fairy further away. Give yourself a three-day vacay and start fresh. 2) Do a brain dump. Stream of conscious writing can be quite illuminating. Set a timer for 15-20 minutes and write anything that pops into your head. This often "unclogs" the mind and shows you what's blocking your progress.

V. **Roadblock Number Five** <u>Fear/Doubt</u>. Sometimes We use one through four as excuses for this guy here. Fear and doubt kill more dreams and goals than anything else. They say it isn't that brave people *don't* have fear, it's that they operate *in spite* of fear. So, the only advice I have for you here is: be brave. Write, publish, and promote despite fear. You're not alone in this.

VI. **The Final Roadblock** is… You. Sorry, but there's no other way to say it. You're roadblocking yourself. Also, I'm kind of an asshole, because this number six is really number one, two, three, four, and five. So much for hating fluff and nonsense, huh? All that stuff up there is the winding way of saying you're in your own way. Do this thing that you say you want to do. Write your book. Today. Now.

Since the name of this chapter is WRITE, let's dig into that. One of the best things you can do for yourself as a writer, is to design your writing routine. Assess how and when you do your best work, where is most conducive to do your writing, and how much time you can allot on a daily (or weekly) basis. Also, decide on a realistic word count goal.

Using myself as an example: I typically write six days a week, from about nine-thirty A.M. until about two P.M. I aim to write at least two-thousand words per day. I have a home office, in which my desk faces the window overlooking the garden and pond. I play music softly in the background because I find it inspiring.

I learned this from some pret-ty famous authors— Stephen King and J.K. Rowling, to name a couple—and it seems to work rather well for them, so… yeah. I realize not all of us have the luxury of such time allowances, so you'll have to find that right pocket of time for you. Even if you can only spare twenty-five minutes out of your day, it's twenty-five minutes more of writing than you did before. It counts.

I emphasize the word routine. This is critical for meeting an end goal before you're one hundred. Get your calendar or you schedule out and pencil it in. Write down your daily/weekly goals and make them realistic and practical. Then check those bad boys off as you accomplish them. Progress is the ultimate motivator.

Once you've established your writing routine, you'll need to understand what kind of writer you are. In our world, you're typical either a plotter or a pantser (and yes, you can be a little of both). A plotter will do things like outline and map out their manuscript, do their research and compile notes, have chapters written out of order, but in folders for later organizing. Whereas a pantser will just sit down and write. I am the latter. I let the story tell itself and travel along with it. Knowing your writing style will help determine your tasks as you write.

> "A writer is someone for whom writing is more difficult than it is for other people."
> — Thomas Mann, Essays of Three Decades

7 Elements of A Story

The very best thing you can ever do for yourself as a writer is to read. Read. Read. Read. Reading will help you become a better writer.

Read books within your genre or topic, read books about writing, read anything and often.

What I strive for with each new book, is to improve as a writer and storyteller. I want each one to be written better than the last. Now, as far as the actual story being told, my success is subjective. Some people have and will like one book and dislike another. What I can say with confidence, is my writing has

improved. Good writing will keep your reader reading, even if the story is meh. Not that we ever think our own story is meh. We wouldn't invest our figurative (and sometimes literal) blood, sweat, and tears on writing it if we did. So, let's break down what makes for a good story. There are eight elements to a story. They are:

- **Setting**: Where and when the story is set.
- **Character**: Who your story is about.
- **Plot**: What your story is about. (this is the arc of your story- introduction, action, conclusion)
- **Conflict**: What the obstacle/challenge/problem is in the story. Without conflict, your story has no real purpose.
- **Theme**: The WHY of the story.
- **Point of View** (POV): Who is telling the story? Be consistent.
- **Tone**: The overall feel or vibe of the story. For example, is it humorous or sad?
- **Style**: How the story is told. For example, if you're writing a story set in the old Wild West, your characters probably won't be speaking in a Boston accent or using words like "dude."

8 ELEMENTS OF A STORY

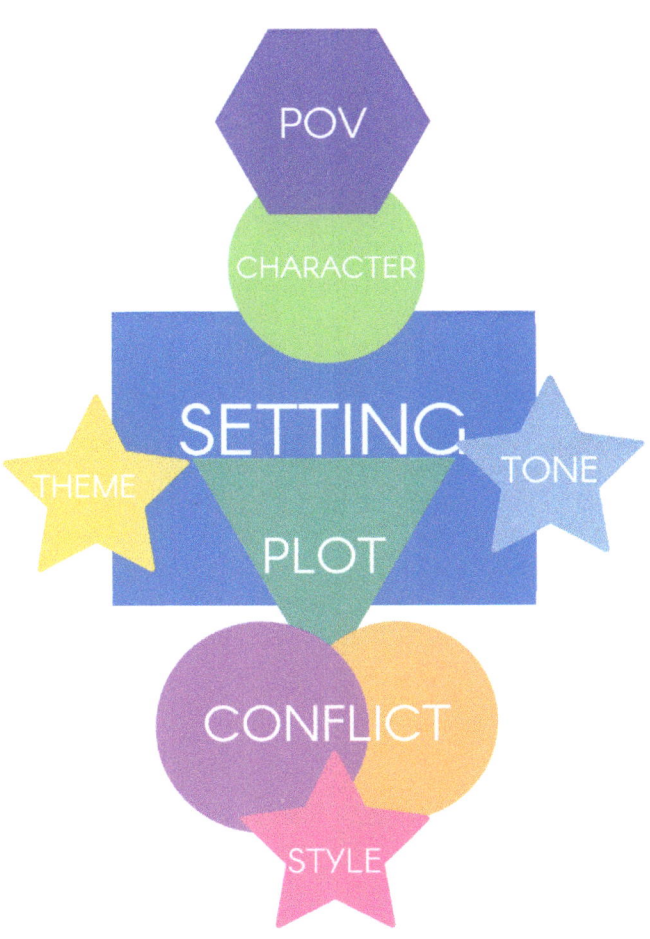

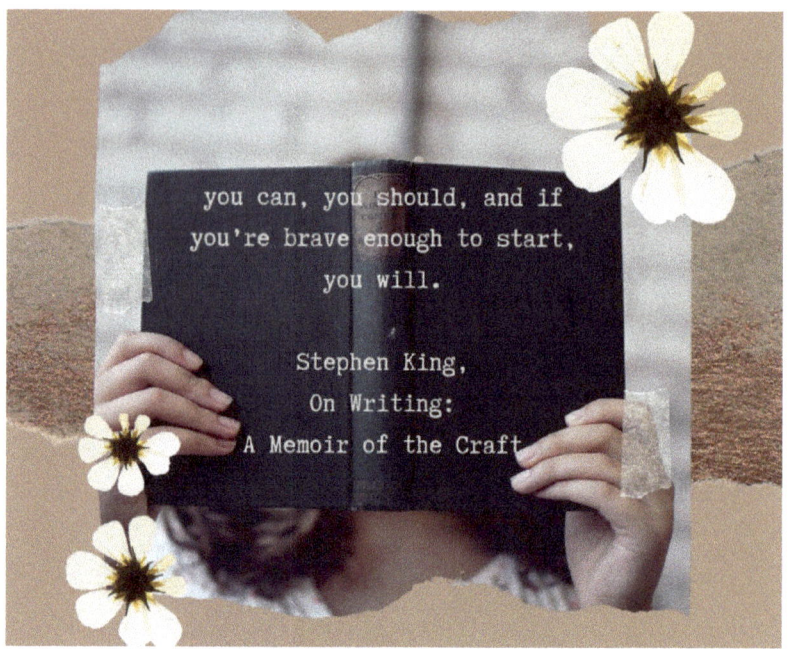

8 Inside the Outline

I don't outline. There, I've confessed. I'm a hardcore, all-out pantser. I sit, I write, I watch the story unfold in front of me. Therefore, my outlining advice comes not from me, but from people who actually outline their books before writing them. First… about that time I DID outline (sort of) and how it worked out.

So, in fairness, I wouldn't call it a fail. Not at all, really. When I began work on the second book in a three-book series (a now set-aside project, cue facepalm) I needed to reacquaint myself with the characters, settings, and so on. I also needed it visible for quick reference, so I went old-school and chose index cards on a corkboard. I propped that big boy behind my laptop, and boom, there it was. Now - and once again, due to my pantser nature - I found it time-consuming and therefore, frustrating. I just want to write, damn it! nd yet, I tried again. Same scenario in writing my series, Welcome to Chance. With more than a dozen "main" characters, there is no choice but to do some outlining. In this case, though, it was more about keeping my characters, um, characteristics, straight. This time I created a People and Places of Chance File and use it for reference. I'm terrible at updating it, so now that I'm thinking of it, I guess I'd better get at it. Damn.

No right or wrong, but consider trying try both ways, or even a hybrid of both, which is very common (especially when writing series). This will all depend on what kind of writer you are: plotter or pantser? Time to get back to writing. Oh, well after I update that character outline. Sigh.

As for you, my more organized friend, outlining your book may be appealing and helpful to you. There are quite a few different methods you could employ, and your choice depends upon your own style of processing and using information. An online book template may be the simplest way to go for most, but if you're someone who works better with tangible visuals, a storyboard might be your friend. If you're an ultra-organized list maker type, you may prefer segmenting your outline chapter by chapter. You see, there really is no right or wrong. Try different outline methods to discover what works best for you. Or, be a pantser like me and just let the story flow. Kidding aside, I do recommend you try it. You just might be a pantser and not even know it!

> "START WRITING, NO MATTER WHAT. THE WATER DOES NOT FLOW UNTIL THE FAUCET IS TURNED ON."
> — LOUIS L'AMOUR

9 Dust, Vacuum, & Polish (AKA: Editing)

But how? That is the question I hear often. Once you've written THE END on a manuscript, your first step in editing is: Walk Away. Yes, seriously. Close it down, stick it in a drawer, step away from the manuscript.

Stephen King has said he leaves it alone for about three weeks. He has more patience than I. Typically I only make it one to two weeks before I start my first round.

I do six rounds of edits, each time looking for a different issue. (My "helper" is a program called Pro-Writing Aid. I have also used Grammarly in the past, as well.) What I look for is as follows:

- Unnecessary/overused words. Listen, I'm wordy and I admit it. I've had to train myself to use less to say more (or the same). Example:
    o Original: "She thought that she was just
- going to have to get off of the floor herself."
    o Revised: "She'd have to get off the floor on her own."
- Also, words such as: just, that, put, very, many, good, great, went, and right tend to appear excessively. Finding and replacing (or removing them) leads to more concise writing.
- Words that tell rather than show. This is one you've likely heard often. Show don't tell. How? Here's an example.
    o Kate saw him moving closer to her. She though he might kiss her. She felt her heart thump wildly.
    o He moved closer. *Oh, my God, I think he's going to kiss me.* Her heart thumped wildly.
- Example B places the reader inside the action, while example A tells the reader about the event, making them a bystander to the action. Giving the character an internal dialogue is a great way to "get around" telling. To tell less and show more, look for words like: know (knows, known, knew), saw (see, seen, sees) want (wanted, wants), feel (feels, felt), and so on. Replace or remove them as much as possible and appropriate. Watch those adverbs outside of dialogue, too.
- Spelling, grammar, and punctuation. Self-explanatory, right?
- Overused phrases. Not unlike overused words, we all tend to have "go to" phrases that may become tiresome to the reader's eye. Here's where we kill our darlings, as the saying goes.

- Thesaurus. This is the, hmm, is there a better way to say that, phase.
- Read aloud. This is a critical, all-important, must-do step. Even after all those previous steps, the read aloud stage will still find mistakes, and usually a lot of them. You'll also hear what your dialogue actually sounds like. Often, it's not as great as we thought it was in our head. Do not skip this step!

It is only after all these steps that I am ready to pass the manuscript onto new

eyes. What many authors do, including myself, is use Beta Readers. A beta reader is a secondary person—preferably an avid book reader with a keen eye and an ability to critique rather than criticize or correct—who is willing to read your book before you publish.

Often, and even after you've combed through your manuscript a million times, your beta readers will still find mistakes, inconsistencies, and sometimes even plot holes. So, even if you are so positive you caught everything, you're wrong. You didn't. How do I know this? Because, 1) I've thought so, too, and was wrong. 2) Famous authors and their teams of paid professionals have been wrong, and had books go to print with errors.

I won't lie. When I find a mistake in a book by a famous author, I'm not-so-secretly thrilled. It's not because I want anyone to fail or feel embarrassed, but rather to remind myself to chill out. To err is human, right?

Or, as I like to say: shit happens. Mistakes get through. You say oops, sorry, fix them, and move on. If you are self-publishing, you may want to hire a professional editor for the very final round of editing. I recommend doing so. A reputable, qualified editor will only make your manuscript better. However, I forewarn you, you're going to find that someone with the credentials you seek is expensive. If you can find it in your budget, do so.

If a professional editor is not within your financial abilities, all is not for naught. There are authors (publishers and editors) out there who'll hate me for writing this, but yes, you can publish a worthy book without the aid of an editor. You just must work harder and know your craft especially well. Don't shortcut, sidestep, or shirk that responsibility.

> WHEN YOUR STORY IS READY FOR REWRITE, CUT IT TO THE BONE. GET RID OF EVERY OUNCE OF EXCESS FAT. THIS IS GOING TO HURT; REVISING A STORY DOWN TO THE BARE ESSENTIALS IS ALWAYS A LITTLE LIKE MURDERING CHILDREN, BUT IT MUST BE DONE.
> — STEPHEN KING —

10 To Self-Publish

This section is devoted to self-publishing. If you've decided—or are just considering—this publishing route, I'll attempt to give you the pros and cons as I see them. As a primarily a self-published author, I have a fair amount of experience with this platform, however, only you can decide what's best for you.

I love self-publishing. It is my preference over traditional publishing. Here is why:

- **Control**. I like having all the control over my work. From inception to cover design, blurb to marketing plan; it's all mine.

- **Enjoyment**. I love each separate phase of creating a book. And believe me, there are a lot of them. Yes, I'll break them down a little later.
- **Ego**. Yeah, that's part of the equation. I do get a sense of pride when I say I did that. All of it.
- **Financial Control and Gain**. Less people involved equals more money in my pocket. You'll be sickened to learn how little you make off each book sale.

Those four factors sum up why I love self-publishing. If they resonate with you and you can relate to those sentiments, then self-publishing might be for you. Better yet: even if you don't want to do all the things, but you still want to self-publish, you can pay someone to do the parts you don't want (or can't) do.

*If you find yourself in the position of weighing self-publishing against publishing through a small publishing house, know that you will still be doing the lion's share of promoting. There's only so much a small publisher can and will do for you. Also, you'll be paying them more per author copy of your book than through (for example) Kindle Direct Publishing (my platform of choice for self-publishing).

So, without knowing you or your skillset, I can't recommend what's best for you. What I can say, is that you have to love, or learn to love, the parts that make up the whole and be prepared to give yourself a crash course in... everything. Yes, and again, I love all the things. You might not.

Based on those factors, why would you *not* want to self-publish? Here you go:

- **Responsibility**. Along with control, comes the burden of responsibility. There's no passing the buck. You wear all the hats: writer, editor (or person who finds editor), cover designer (person who hires cover designer), publisher, marketer/promoter, website designer (or person...you know) social media handler, booking agent... you see what I'm saying? *All the hats*.

- **Tediousness**. Instead of just writing your damn book, you're doing all the little things. Usually while complaining that all you want to do is just write, damn it.

- **Blame**. Not unrelated to responsibility, doing all the things also means it's on you if the formatting is wonky, or there's glaring mistakes, or your cover is sub-par.

- **You Work Harder**. See the above and compare with this: An author with a publisher writes the book, turns it over, approves the edits and the cover they provide (at no cost to the author) and does as much or as little self-promoting as they chose.

If You're Saying, Yep Self-Publishing Is For Me...

For the sake of this section, let's say you want to self-publish. But how, exactly? At the time of publishing this book, there are ten "top" self-publishing platforms. They all offer a variation of the same things. For the purpose of speaking on only what I personally know from my experiences, I'll discuss the two platforms I use: Kindle Direct Publishing and Ingram Spark. As with any brand or company I mention throughout, I receive no compensation whatsoever from them to advertise or promote the products or services. Unfortunately.

Kindle Direct Publishing. This service is from Amazon and is beyond easy to use. Oh, and it is free. Yes, free. No strings attached thus far. You simply sign up (or use your existing Amazon account information to sign up) and follow their steps to publish your manuscript.

*Need more help? Watch My Video at elsakurt.com

First, the steps for a paperback. The steps—broken up into three panels--are as simple as inserting the name of your book, accepting their *free ISBN number (you must have an ISBN to publish your book for distribution) or supplying your own.
***I highly recommend buying your own ISBN through Bowker**. With your own ISBN, you'll be able to publish your book on multiple platforms using that same ISBN, whereas using KDP's locks you into using only theirs.
Supply the publisher name (yourself or the imprint you've created) as well as author name (your own or your pen name) and all other pertinent information about your book.
Pick your trim size (most typical are 5 x 8 or 6 x 9) and paper color (cream is default and best choice). Upload your manuscript and cover image. You will upload a PDF in both cases, or—for cover design—use their free cover creator tool. I DO NOT recommend using cover images offer by KDP. These are stock photos, usable by anyone, and the odds of seeing the same book cover image on another book

are high. Use your own high-quality image or hire a designer to create one for you.

Lastly, determine your book price and markets for distribution. This is a simplified break-down of a relatively simple process.

There are some other questions along the way that, if you don't know the answer, they offer prompts with suggestions and explanations.

For Uploading an Ebook…

For uploading an ebook, KDP has made this process just as easy, if not easier. If you are creating both ebook and paperback at the same time, KDP will link the formats so that when you click the box to start inputting your book information, the fields populate with the info you used for the paperback.

KDP has also been kind enough to offer a free ebook formatting service called Kindle Create. If you download the program, you'll be able to upload your document (manuscript) and format it to look its best on their Kindle readers. You can only use this for your ebooks being published through KDP. If you want to make your ebooks available on other formats (Apple Books, Google Play books, ect.) you'll need copies in either .mobi or epub. Again, offering your books on as many platforms as possible can only benefit you, however, it's not required.

A note of importance: If you plan of publishing your book on more than one platform (either ebook or print version) DO NOT check the box for expanded distribution on KDP.

Other Platforms…

Once I've set up my book on Amazon, I move onto Ingram Spark, and do the same. You can do this in reverse order, I don't believe there is a right or wrong. Ingram Spark's setup is not quite as easy as KDP's, however, it is still relatively easy and fast. There is also a setup fee with Ingram Spark, but discount codes are often available through a quick internet search.

Why both? Publishing through KDP, which is under the Amazon umbrella, places your books on the Mack daddy of online retailers. It doesn't get much bigger than Amazon, folks. It's a no brainer, really. Get your books on the biggest, fastest delivering service out there (that I know of, at least). You might wonder why that isn't enough.

So Why Isn't It Enough?

Brick and mortar stores and libraries view Amazon as direct competition and a threat to their livelihood. They generally will not buy from them, which means your books won't go on their shelves. So, where do they go for their books, then?

Well, Ingram (and Baker & Taylor). They are the Mack daddy of bookstores and libraries. Aside from getting to "stick it" to Amazon, retailers who use Ingram to buy books for their stores enjoy the perks of discount purchasing and being able to return unsold books at no cost or loss to them. Does that mean you, as the author/publisher of your books on Ingram Spark, must mark your books as returnable and offer a discount?

Ultimately, no... but yes, if you want a higher probability of retailers buying your books for sale in their stores.

11 The Nutshell

No matter what platform you choose, be sure to make your book the best it can be, outside and in. A cover that is professional looking and visually striking (or at least interesting) is your gateway. Your blurb is your hook. And your well-written, well-edited content is what fuels recommendations and drives future sales. Be prepared to answer these questions (to yourself)

- Am I willing and able to take on the burden (and thrill!) of responsibility for all aspects of my writing journey?

- Do I have—or am I willing to learn—the skills needed to do so?

- Can I say with pride that I am self-published, or will I feel less than someone who is traditionally published?

"AND BY THE WAY, EVERYTHING IN LIFE IS WRITABLE ABOUT IF YOU HAVE THE OUTGOING GUTS TO DO IT, AND THE IMAGINATION TO IMPROVISE. THE WORST ENEMY TO CREATIVITY IS SELF-DOUBT."
— SYLVIA PLATH

PATH TO AUTHORSHIP

12 To Traditionally Publish

There's no question about it. Getting to say the words, "I'm traditionally published," or "My publisher..." are a big deal in our world. What it tells the world is that someone other than your mom or your best friend thinks your work has value. It's a great feeling. It validates you as a writer. I love being able to say it just as much as I love being a self-published author. You're going to find in this industry that there are those who look down their noses at anyone who is self-published. Their arguments—in fairness—have some merit.

When I say anyone can publish a book, I mean anyone can publish a book. This means some sincere garbage has gone out into the universe for public consumption and ridicule. Although—also in fairness—there have been books published through publishing companies that could arguably considered garbage, too. Eye of the beholder, I suppose.

My Two Cents

When asked, I tell people I believe there is room for everyone. I believe this sincerely. However, we are only talking about traditional publishing in this section. Let's start with the pros of having a publisher.

- Bragging rights. See the previous page.
- Having an editor (that you don't have to pay for).
- Having a cover designer (that you don't have to pay for).
- Having someone else handle the details.

Cons of Traditional Publishing

- You are beholden for the length of your contract. If you're not happy with the direction they took your book, you're (kind of) stuck.
- You lose control over parts of your book. Listen, they're not monsters and they're not trying to destroy what you've created, but their vision might not match yours and you might be stuck with their choices.
- You'll pay more for your author copies than what you would through (for example)

KDP. Your publisher is going to try to make money off you any way they can. It's a business, after all.

Side Note

The number one thing you must know is this: A real publishing company will never ask you to pay for any part of the publishing process. EVER. If a so-called publisher tells you to pay an upfront fee to produce your book, they are not a publisher, they are a glorified printer. A common term for this practice is "vanity press." All they are doing for you is what you can do for yourself on KDP and charging you—usually an insane amount—for it. Trust me, stay away.

The Big Five

Let's talk about the Big Five. They are **Hachette, HarperCollins, Macmillan, Penguin Random House and Simon & Schuster**. Without a literary agent, you cannot submit your manuscript to them. *You may, however, be able to submit to one of their hundreds of imprints. If this is your goal—publishing with one of the big five—then prepare to spend a considerable amount of time querying literary agents. It's a tedious and stressful process and involves a LOT of rejection emails. Might you be the exception to the rule? Sure. But best to mentally prepare for otherwise.

If your goal is to simply get a traditional publishing company to publish your book, your luck improves. There are quite a few of smaller presses out there that are open to un-agented submissions.

Technically Speaking…

When submitting your work to a publishing house, you MUST follow their instructions/guidelines EXACTLY. If they say Times New Roman, 12 pt font, do NOT send them your MS in Calibri 11 pt. If they say to send the first three chapters in the body of your email, and not as an attachment, DO NOT ATTACH your first three chapters… or send them more than what they asked for, even if the best part comes in at chapter four. The only exception is when your chapters are short, and they will make a note of that in their terms.

Typically, They'll Request…

- Times New Roman,
- 12 pt font,
- Single-spaced.
- Word count & genre.
- Brief letter of query where you'll summarize (including ending) your story, what (if any) current popular books on the market it's comparable to, and a little about you.
- First three to five chapters.

*There are exceptions and variations, and some publishers may ask for the whole manuscript. Do not submit unless your MS is COMPLETE and edited!

You'll either send these as one (or several) attachments, or within the body of the email itself, or within their generated drop-in form. Regardless of their specifications, it will be made clear by each individual company.

About Those Query Letters…

Sigh. I've yet to meet a single soul who enjoys writing them. Honestly? The suck. Tedious, stressful, frustrating. But if they're done right and done well, you've got a shot. Aside from the number one rule – follow instructions – the next best things I can tell you are: Be authentic. Let your true self come out. Be succinct. How you write in your query letter is their indication of how you write as an author. It's important to convey exactly what you're about, how you view your work, and that you have a clear idea of where it fits in the universe. Be confident, not cocky i.e.: "The underlying message of the story truly speaks to the current climate of our society right now," and NOT, "If you pass on this amazing, awesome story, you're crazy. It's the best thing since Pride and Prejudice." They'll often want to know what book(s) you'd compare yours to.

My Suggestions…

- Follow their submission guidelines to a T. If they ask for the first five chapters in the body of your email, do not attach the file. And vice versa. Not following the rules will get your submission unopened and deleted, guaranteed, even if it's a masterpiece.
- Submit only when you are positive it is the absolute best it can be. That means typo free, too.
- If you're not sure what to say in your query, look up sample query letters online for tips. Don't wing it.
- Write a compelling blurb and (if asked for one) give a clear synopsis of the book in as few words as reasonable. This is the publishers first look at what kind of writer

you are. If you bore them with the blurb, you've lost them. Be patient. It's not unusual for months to go by with no word. Don't pester them after the first week.
- Be gracious. Rejections happen; it's part of the game. If they say your manuscript isn't what they're looking for at this time, thank them and move on.
- Educate yourself. When that contract comes through, read it thoroughly and consider a lawyer's input for anything you don't understand.

Things To Know

Know that a small publishing house may not have the resources to promote your book in the ways you imagined when signing that publishing contract. You will likely be your own marketer. In fact, they'll expect it of you.

There are many variations of the above. Each company will have their own spin on things, but generally they operate the same way. You will be giving up parts of your book—such as cover design—and some editing decisions.

You'll have input, but they'll have final say. Once again, only you can decide what you're willing to compromise on.

This is in no way meant to discourage you from seeking a publisher, but rather to make you aware of the realities. The reality is, having a publisher can potentially open doors you'd only hoped for when starting out. The reality is also that having a publisher is not all it cracked up to be.

13 The Nutshell

When you've reached this point in your journey, take the time and effort to research and learn about the options available to you. Make your own pros and cons list. Ask yourself questions like:

- How soon would I like to see my work published?

- Can I wait for the "right" offer to come along?

- Can I handle the inevitable rejections, or will it discourage me to a point where I discard the project?

- Am I okay with giving up control over aspects of my book?

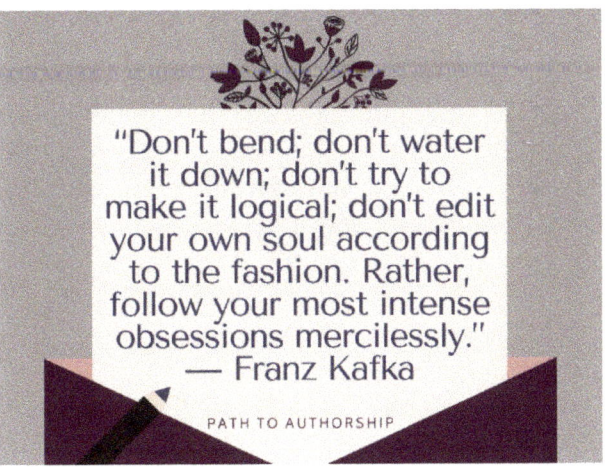

14 Next Steps

For the sake of continuity, let's say your manuscript is complete, edited, proofread, your book cover is exactly what you've envisioned it would be, and you've chosen your publishing lane. Congratulations. The next steps are no less intimidating than the previous, I'm afraid. However, if you have a plan, it's much easier. So, let's make a plan (in the form of a checklist).

- Write the book (CHECK!)
- Edit (CHECK!)
- Choose publishing option (CHECK!)
- Develop a marketing plan, including but not limited to marketing book via social media presence building (WAIT, WHAT?)

Don't stress. It's actually not that bad. We'll start with building your social media/online presence. Whether you love social media, hate it, or are somewhere in between, the simple fact is, is that it's the fastest, cheapest, and easiest way to get your content out to the world. While I encourage you to "claim" your author name on all the major social media platforms, I also say you don't have to use them all. Pick the one you like (or are most competent at) and direct your focus there. The "major" social media platforms are Facebook, Twitter, Instagram, Pinterest, and Snapchat. If you have a profile on at least the first three, you'll give yourself a fighting chance out there in the wild.

First: I recommend having a website to direct potential readers to. It doesn't have to be content rich and can be quite basic. An "about me" page (or paragraph if using a single page layout), an "about my book" (along with image(s) of your book) page, and links to buy the book. Also, consider blogging on your website as an additional way to pull interest to you and your work. This is a nice way for potential readers to get to know you and your writing style.

Second: Create a public/community/author profile on Facebook, Instagram, and/or Twitter (and any others you like). Use the same profile picture, handle, and cover photo for all. For example, I am @authorelsakurt on all platforms, and my profile picture is the same on each. This is for easy recognizability. When you tell someone to "check me out on social media," you want it to be easy for them to find.

Side Note Regarding Social Media

What should you post on social media? Fun, thoughtful, engaging posts that are not always "buy my book" pitches. It your book is about a specific topic or location, share interesting tidbits or photos about it. Ask your audience topical questions (not politics or any other "hot button" topic unless you're prepared for a shitstorm). Often, the silliest thing—like Name Your Top Five Movies of All Time—gets the most engagements. Always use eye-catching graphics and/or videos. This—engagements—is the name of the social media game. You're looking for likes, shares, and comments in order to increase your page's visibility.

Each social media platform has its own style. Facebook attracts an older demographic and is fond of memes, GIFs, and videos, whereas Instagram is image and hashtag heavy. It will serve you well to watch some tutorials on how these platforms work.

I use a social media calendar, which can be found in my 4 Must Have Resources for Writers at elsakurt.com

Back to our steps...

Third. Set up your author profiles on Goodreads, Amazon Author Central, and BookBub to start. These three drives the most readers to books, so it can only benefit you to be listed on them. There are several other author platforms to add your book(s) to, as well.

Do you have to do these things, and why? Yes... and no. When considering that Amazon alone carried forty-eight and a half million books on their site, you may have a clearer understanding of just how many other people are trying to do the same thing you are doing. If you want to give your book a chance to be seen—and since you've taken the time to write and publish it, I think you do—you need put it in front of readers.

Once you've set yourself up on the various platforms, you'll want to give them a reasonable amount of attention. Posting one to three times a day on your primary social media platform (mine is Facebook currently) is sufficient.

As for your author profile pages on Goodreads, Amazon Author Central, and BookBub, they are a must-have, and all you'll need to do is have your (published book(s) listed, along with an interesting author bio and blurb about your book. You'll be encouraging and reminding your social media followers to follow those pages, as well.

If you're thinking, "Okay, but what if I really hate the idea of social media?" Well, then, a newsletter is your best alternative. In fact, offering a newsletter to your readers/followers is highly recommended whether you use social media or not. Building your subscriber list is a wonderful way to share your content quickly and easily with the world.

WRITE>>PUBLISH>>PROMOTE
A TIMELINE

Write!
At About the 3/4 Finish Point:
- create website & social media pages & begin liking and following pages in the writing community
- begin adding content to website and social media
- begin cover design process (if self-publishing)

At Completion of First Draft Of Manuscript
- have business cards & all other marketing materials designed and ordered.
- continue building interest and excitement for your upcoming book release (announce launch date, do a cover reveal, live video to discuss the book, ect)

One -Three Months Before Publishing
- find a launch party site. (bookstore, library, coffee shop, winery... the possiblities are many!)
- create a social media post to invite friends, family, acquaintances, and anyone who loves books (particularly your genre) to your party
- plan to offer a prize or giveaway (gift basket typically) to a lucky guest as incentive to come out.

Three weeks - One Month Before Official Launch Date
- order copies of your book. Fifty to one hundred is a safe bet.post regularly to social media about upcoming launch.
- contact your local community newpaper reporter and ask them to do a story on you.
- write a press release and publish to your local papers.
- order a credit card reader (or download an app to accept credit cards)

One Week - Day Before Launch Party
- share a daily countdown to launch party
- gather all items for launch
- visit your launch site to check in
- breathe. it's all going to be fine.

15 Newsletters

Starting and Building A Subscriber List. Can you use your regular email to send out newsletters? Sure… but why on earth would you? Even the least tech savvy person can learn how to use a service like Mailchimp or Mailer Lite.
Why Use A Service?

- Reason 1) Once you've set up your templates, you can just drag, drop, and type in your content.
- 2) It looks way more professional.
- 3) It's a separate entity from your regular email, therefore more manageable.
- 4) Did I mention it is way more professional looking?

Since I use Mailchimp currently, I'll talk more specifically about their offerings.
Starting: As with many programs out there now, Mailchimp will walk you through set up. It is a free service up to two thousand subscribers. Using their templates, you can create attractive newsletters for your followers with pictures, links, and more. Their options are many and varied and include the ability to have an automatic welcome email sent to new subscribers.
Building. There's one rule about building your subscriber list: You can't just randomly start sending emails to people without their permission. Meaning, you can't just add everyone in your personal email list to the subscriber list. You have to ask them either in person or (ironically) via email (if you know them well). It really is as simple as asking people to subscribe, or for their email address. How Not to Ask: "Hey, can I get you to join my email list?" A Better

Way to Ask: "Don't forget to sign up for my newsletter to find out_____" The blank can be whatever you're offering. Whether its, "…about my top-secret recipe for banana bread" or "…my latest giveaway," always have something to entice people to want to subscribe. People love to win things, so giveaways (a chance to win a free ebook or a signed copy) are always a great incentive.

What to Write: Newsletters should be fun, engaging, informative, and brief. Make is professional, but with a touch of personal. I usually give a recap (with pictures) of the previous month's events, a look at what's coming up, and that month's giveaway. I also give them exclusive, subscriber only content like sneak peeks at my WIP or inside info. They get first chances to buy my newest books, or I give them bonus stories. When in doubt, the internet is your friend. You can easily find tutorials, samples, and suggestions for creating a newsletter.

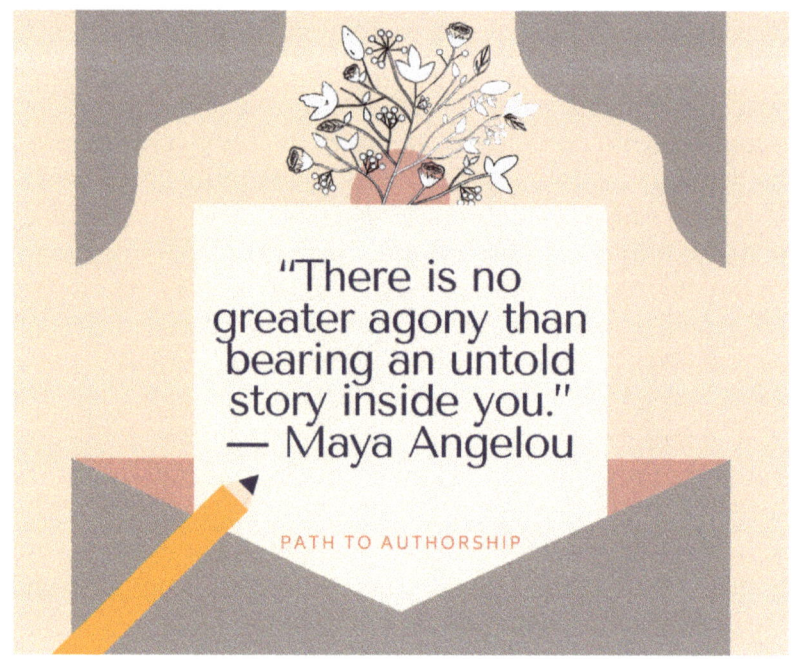

16 Putting Yourself Out There

This part is daunting to even the most extroverted among us. For us introverts, it's downright horrifying… initially. It gets easier, I promise. In fairness, you can do as much or as little as you want in promoting yourself and your book. If you wrote it to simply check it off your bucket list and call it done, that's totally fine. If you just want to casually bring it up to people at parties or sell it (or give it away) to your friends and family, also okay.

However, if you are avoiding the task of putting yourself out there because you're afraid or embarrassed, that's less okay. Here's a little tough love for you: Stand up straight and get that chin out. You just did something millions of other people only dream about (or say they're going to do, but never do). You wrote a book, damn it, and that is way cool. You're no longer just a writer, you're an author. Holy shit, right?!

Hard Facts. Yes, some people will not like your book. And those people might review your book negatively. You'll need to adopt the *can't please everyone* attitude and shake it off. That's not to say you can't have a poor me moment, of course. I call it the Five-Minute Pity Party and I totally recommend it. Get that timer out and allow yourself to feel all the feels, eat the Haagen Dazs (because you deserve the good stuff), and wallow. And, yes, it can be longer than five minutes. Hell, give yourself a day. But by all means—literally or mentally—set a timer on that pity party, and when the timer goes off, get up and get going. The path to success is paved with failure, my friends.

I, like many authors, avoid reading reviews. Ironically, I regularly request and hope for them just as much as I dread them. The reality is, they're not for my eyes anyhow; they are for readers. Books, like most things in life, are subjective. One person's trash is another's treasure, and so on. I had someone call my writing pretentious. Another found it charming. It is what it is. All we can do is write what feels right to us. To paraphrase Toni Morrison, write a book you'd want to read.

Happy Facts. There are people like you who want to read your book. There are people like you who've written books like yours, and have suffered the same doubts, worries, and fears you do. There are people like you who took a chance on themselves despite those fears. These people are your tribe, and they are the ones you focus on. While writing may be one of the most isolating endeavors, the writing community is a wealth of camaraderie and support.

If you haven't done so yet, this is a great time to start building your own writer/author tribe. Connecting with others in the vast writing community is a terrific way to expand your platform, increase visibility, and thereby find more opportunities to make more sales. Some ways for new authors to do this are:

- Join a local writer's group or book club.
- Join/Follow social media pages or handles that discuss and/or promote books and authors.
- Create your own group and invite fellow writers/authors to join.
- Become active in your community.
- Attend book signings and events for authors.

17 The Nutshell

The above was something I resisted early on—all this people-ing—but when I finally started getting out there, I discovered tremendous value, emotionally and career-wise, in it. At least half of what I've learned has been through my engagement with the writing community and has helped me grow as a writer, self-promoter, and mentor to new and aspiring authors. Get out there! Grab a buddy, if it helps, and start networking. You'll be glad you did.

A common hurdle we face is a sneaky bastard called Imposter Syndrome. It's a false belief - a little voice in our heads - telling us we aren't good enough, talented enough, or smart enough to be doing this. If this is something you struggle with, check out my post about it my blog and learn how to overcome it.

18 Now What?

    Your book is out (or just about to be out) in the universe. But here's the thing: It can't market itself, so that means it's up to you to get that book in readers hands. Having it available on your website or Amazon isn't enough. Here's where we have to put on our big girl and big boy pants and ask retailers to carry our books on their shelves. There are a few ways to do this.

    In person. If you decide to go into a bookstore to ask them to carry your book, it should only be AFTER you've visited their website and looked for a) their policy and procedure for doing so, b) and get a feel for their store. Generally, it is frowned upon to just walk in off the street and give your pitch to the store owner/manager. On the flip side, it's not unusual for busy stores to miss over overlook your inquiry, and it requires either a follow up email, or that walk-in.

If, for whatever reason, you decide to pay the store a visit (because, yes, it
is harder to say no to someone in person) have a plan of approach ready.

Prepare for either of the following scenarios:

- The store owner/manager is busy. Do not try to pitch someone when they have customers. Ever. At most, wait for a reasonable opportunity to say, "Hey, I can see you're super busy, so I'd just like to drop this off to you." Hand over a copy of your book (if available) and a business card with your contact info. "When you have some time, I'd really appreciate a chance to talk to you about carrying my book in your store." Thank them for their time, buy something in the store, and get out of their hair.
- The store owner/manager is available to chat. Compliment the store and apologize for coming in unannounced. Have your book in hand (if available), along with a business card or info postcard for the book. Briefly and enthusiastically say who you are, whether you're a local author, and why you/your book is a great fit for their store.

What To Say

Consider something like this: "Hi, I'm sure you're super busy, but I just wanted to stop by and introduce myself. I'm Elsa, and I'm a local author with a new book coming out in two weeks. I would love if you'd consider carrying it here at_____." If you've intrigued them, or even if they're just being polite, they'll let you go on and/or ask some leading questions. One of the things they may ask, is if you plan on having a book launch and, if so, where. Conversely, this may be something you bring up to them. If you'd like them to host your book launch, say so. Then, tell them how you plan on drawing customers into the store.

Draw Them In

Um, so how will you draw them in? Here's where we circle back to social media, our website, and the connections we've made in the community. Hopefully, you've been telling anyone and everyone about your upcoming/newly released book. Now you'll put them to work, too. Ask them to share, share, share. Word of mouth should never be underestimated. Maybe even throw in an incentive, like, "Spread the word about my book launch for a chance to win a signed copy! Simply, LIKE, SHARE, and COMMENT on this post and I'll chose a winner on____" or something similar. The more people who know about your event, the better your turnout.

But What If They Don't Come?

Listen. It happens. You do all the things, you think happy thoughts, and prepare to the nth degree... and no one comes (or very few). Yes, it's painful. But the good news is, we've all been there. It's nothing personal against you. It's just life. Book signings by unknown authors are not a big draw, generally speaking. You'll probably get a great first turnout thanks to your friends and family, but after that... not so much. It takes time and effort to build buzz and interest in you and your book. Keep at it.

20 THINGS YOU'LL NEED FOR A BOOK SIGNING

1. **Books**. Depending on the venue, between 20-50 is a safe number. However, best practice is to have more in the car for just in case.
2. **Pen**. I know, duh, right? You'de be surprised how many of us forget the damn pen. Have a few, and make sure they're not "runners"
3. **Tablecloth**. Your venue may supply one, but never assume.
4. **Table & Chair**. And, if it's an outdoor event, a pop-up style canopy! Check with your venue to see if they'll be providing these. If not, bring your own. Average is anywhere from a four foot to six-foot table. Author spaces (at multi-vendor events) are either 8 x 10 feet or 10 x 10
5. A sturdy **utility cart** with wheels to transport your stuff. Believe me, you don't want to lug boxes.
6. Some type of **e-commerce tool** (like a Square card reader) for credit card purchases. Consider offering PayPal and/or Venmo options, too.
7. **Change**. Dollar bills, fives, and tens. I usually price my books in even increments ($10, $15) with the sales tax built in to avoid dealing with coins.
8. **Price labels or a sign** displaying book price (s) & if you accept credit cards.
9. **Bags**. Don't forget bags for your customers!
10. **Bookstands** (frame/plate holders work well)
11. **Banner/Signage**. You need something eye-catching that announces who you are and what you're selling!
12. **Business cards**. Tell em where to find you, especially if they're not buying today.
13. **Freebies**. Think: bookmarks, pens, magnets, or anything branded with your logo/book.
14. **Candy or chocolates**. Nothing stops em like a treat. A bowl for those chocolates/candies.
15. **Tape**. Just because you never know
16. **Scissors**. See 15.
17. **A snack & beverage**. Depending on the duration of your event. Only on occassion do your hosts think of these things.
18. **Your elevator pitch**. Be ready to talk about your book. Practice it. Don't give the whole synopsis, give the back cover blurb.
19. **A smile and great attitude**. I'm not being snarky here, this is a must. Be approachable. Be friendly. Be engaged. Stand up for longer chats, keep your phone checking at a minimum, and make eye contact.
20. Have a **"catch phrase"** to reel them in. (But don't be obnoxious with it.) Asking what types of books they like to read is a great ice breaker.

19 The Nutshell

As you can see, there are a lot of moving parts when it comes to writing, publishing, and promoting your book. As nice as it would be to have a perfectly linear path, often the lanes intersect or run parallel. This is where referencing your timeline comes in handy. But honestly? Nothing terrible will happen if you forget one thing or another, or if your timeline looks more like a maze than a straight-ish line. I've learned what I know over time, through (many) mistakes, and by trial and error. My "brand" didn't instantly happen; I built it over time, and it evolved. You will, too.

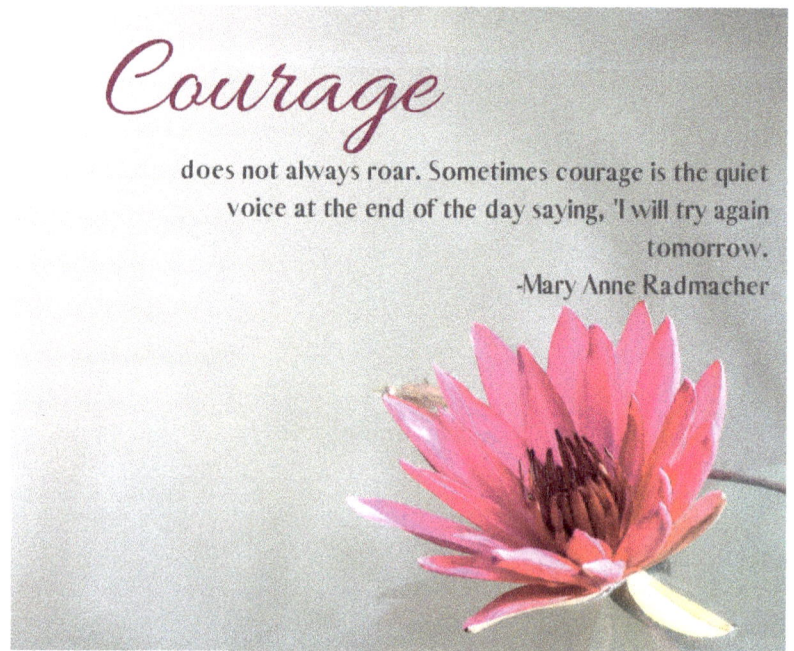

Courage does not always roar. Sometimes courage is the quiet voice at the end of the day saying, 'I will try again tomorrow.
-Mary Anne Radmacher

20 Navigating the Book Selling Circuit

Welcome to the wonderful world of self-promotion. If you've done all (or at least most) of the above, you're ready. This section is broken up in to two parts: the **How To**, and **How to Not**.

So, how do you get your books into more hands in the "real" world (AKA: in-person sales). Well, you get a booth/table at book conventions, book fairs, craft fairs, church fairs, multi-author events, and just about any other kind of public event that accepts authors as vendors. They aren't too hard to find. In fact, they're right at your fingertips via social media. Organizations regularly post upcoming events and if they're looking for vendors. Be sure to like and follow local pages, particularly libraries, churches, bookstores, and so on. In the fall is when you find an abundance of opportunities. Most events charge a vendor fee and have varying requirements, so do your research to see if the event is worth your while. Some considerations when choosing an event:

• Is this an annual event with a good following/customer traffic?

• Is the fee proportionate to that traffic and renown?

• Will my product "fit in" with the event? (i.e. your gruesome horror story or BDSM novel may not be a good fit at a church fair)

• Have any of your author acquaintances vended at this event before, and if so, what did they think?

• Are they advertising and promoting the event?

If the answers to those question satisfy you, then by all means, grab your books and gear, and go for it!

ARE YOU READY TO MAKE YOUR DREAM A REALITY?

21 Congratulations

You're at your first event. Whether it's a book convention or event with multiple authors, a fair/festival, or your own book signing, there are some unwritten "rules" to go by.

Do's and Don'ts:

- **Be prepared**. Have everything you need from your checklist. If you've forgotten your table, chances are, you might be out of luck. Same for your chair.
- **Be approachable**. You'd be surprised at how many authors I've seen sitting with their heads down in their phones or with their arms crossed and a scowl.
- **Be prepared, part two**. Have your "elevator pitch" ready. All this means is that you're

ready to briefly talk about your book. Give them the blurb, basically.
- **Do NOT** summarize the entire book, talk their ear off, or harangue them into buying your book. I've seen it happen, and it is cringeworthy.
- **Be courteous**. Listen, people are sometimes rude. They ask rude questions or make rude comments. Let them go on their way with a smile and little thought.
- **Be professional**.
- **Do NOT** carry on phone conversations when shoppers are nearby or ignore them in favor of a great conversation your having with your neighboring vendor.
- **Be mindful** of your fellow vendors. If you're chatty by nature, maybe tone it down a notch. Everyone is there to sell, not just you. Mindfulness extends to utilizing your allotted space and nothing more, and to respecting your shopper's cues. If they're trying to politely inch away, let them go (but offer a business card in case they want to follow you online).
- **Do NOT** monopolize the shoppers or call them away from another author/vendor.
- **Do** fulfill your obligation to the letter. If the event runs from nine AM to three PM, arrive early for set up and stay until the end.
- **Do NOT** pack up early unless agreed upon with the event coordinator. It is extremely inconsiderate and distracting to those sticking it out.

22 Paid Promoting

Promoting yourself and your book is not a one-time shot. It requires strategy, persistence, and patience. Oh, and money. How much or little is up to you. Some avenues for paid promotion:

- Seek out Blog Tour companies to promote your new release. They usually need about three weeks to a month advance notice. Cost varies & depends on services you choose. I have used a blog tour company with minimal success. This is not to say I I'd discourage you from using one, but just my personal experience.
- Create an Amazon ad through your KDP account. This requires a strong

understanding of keyword use, algorithms, and knowing your target audience. Kindlepreneur is great for learning these things.

      o Boosted social media posts. Again, research and knowledge are key. Don't throw good money away on ads that won't reach anyone who might buy your book.

      o Advertise on Bookbub, Goodreads, AllAuthor, and other book sites. This can be costly, so proceed with caution and, yes, again, knowledge.

Be wary of emails from companies offering to promote your book for you. Vet them to be sure they are legitimate and have a large enough following to be worthwhile. It's also easy to be enticed by sites that offer to increase your followers on social media. It may work temporarily (quick gains but followed by unfollows shortly after) and may even get you booted from the platform. The same can be said for paid review sites. This is a big NO. **We do not pay for reviews**. Read that twice. Yeah, it's tempting. We need reviews to blip on Amazon's radar. They are so hard to come by organically and I deeply envy anyone who gets readers to do it. But paying for reviews is cheating and it's wrong. When you ask for a review, you ask for an *honest* review. Since no one *wants* bad reviews, one way of asking is to say, "If you enjoyed the story, I'd love if you let other readers know by sharing a review on Amazon (or Goodreads, BookbBub, etc..)"

Regardless of what type of promotion you choose, if any, it goes almost without saying that you must promote your work consistently. Know your target audience and focus your energy and attention on them. Join groups and follow pages that appeal to your audience, then become active within the group. This does NOT mean spam them with Buy My Book posts or private message them with sales pitches. Please, don't be *that guy*. It's the fastest way to get blocked and banned and it's just annoying. Instead, leave thoughtful comments, offer helpful advice, and be relatable. If you pique someone's interest, they'll go to your profile learn more and may just reach out to you!

Devote a small block of time each day (or once a week to schedule posts. I use a social media calendar cheat sheet from Angie Gessler) and engage in social media with a businessperson's mindset. This means not engaging in keyboard warrior battles with people you think are idiots. Everything you do reflects your book/brand.

Lastly, don't be afraid to think outside the box when it comes to promoting. If you have a unique or interesting angle or connections, make it work for you. Be creative! Just know your niche. Promoting your BDSM romance novel at the school fair would be an obvious fail, right?

23 The Nutshell

Having good event etiquette increases the likelihood of being invited back and is just overall good karma. Speaking of good karma, recommending your fellow authors is a great practice. Say a reader approaches your table and says they only read mystery novels, but you only write romance. Point him/her down the aisle at your fellow author who writes mystery. It does you no harm, and you can't lose a sale you never made.

On the contrary, it may get you a sale when the mystery author reciprocates the favor!

A stickier issue when attending multi-author events is a common practice of "book trading" between authors. I'm not a fan of the practice in general, and only because it often times is with someone whose genre I never read. Use your own discretion as to whether you'll trade one of your books for someone else's, and if you decline, so as politely and gently as possible.

24 Resources

Since I wish someone had done this for me, I've compiled a collection of resources I've personally used over the years for each phase of my own writing journey. I cannot guarantee your satisfaction.

- **Stephen King**. Okay, first: Stephen. Freaking. King. You don't have to like his work to respect the absolute fact of his success. Reading (or listening on audiobook) his personal journey, absorbing his knowledge and insights, and discovering how relatable his experiences and feelings are on writing… just yes. As a side note, I love the surprisingly (and maybe accidentally) love story woven in throughout the book.
- **The Elements of Style**. Another book I listened to while driving, cooking, cleaning. Sweet Jesus does it come across as pompous.

However, it is in many ways a writer's dictionary of proper writing. You don't have to obey every rule all of the time, but you should know the rules, nonetheless.
- **Bookworks** has grown daily in my esteem. I follow them on Facebook and get a constant supply of great info.
- **Your Local Library**, of course. Enough said, right?
- **Your local/independent bookstores**. Don't just go in when you want them to carry your book. Shop there, support their business, be someone THEY want to support. And don't cold call with your books in hand. Follow the guidelines on their website, always.
- Yep, time to set aside your fear or hatred of **social media** if you're an author. You need them. Author profiles on each of the major platforms, regular posting, and networking with the rest of the writing community can only help you.
- **Kindlepreneur** is one hell of a resource. YouTube tutorials and more all for free when you subscribe. They also run KDP Rocket.
- **Pro Writing Aid**… oh, how I love you. This is a paid for add-on to Microsoft Word and it goes through your manuscript with a fine-tooth comb, checking for everything from punctuation to plagiarism.
- **Udemy** has courses on just about anything you can think of. From marketing to graphic design, writing, publishing on Amazon… hell, you can even take a course for hypnotherapy certification if you want. Another inexpensive resource to further your self-education that I love using.

- **Canva, Canva, Canva**. I use Canva every. Damn. Day. It'll take too long to list everything you can use it for, so suffice to say: all the things (graphics related). From ebook covers to teaser & blurb graphics. Social media graphics & covers… oh, wait, I'm listing, aren't I?! Go check it out. It's 12.99 a month and worth every penny.
- **Grammarly** An AI writing add on for checking your MS for mistakes. There is a free version and a paid.
- **Bluehost** Website hosting. Plenty of others to choose from, though.
- **Wordpress** I've used this website platform one from the beginning. Again, others to choose from.
- **Vistaprint** One stop shop for many marketing needs. Always check for discount/coupon codes!
- **Best of Signs** Same deal as Vistaprint. I've used them for table runners.

PTA QUESTIONNAIRE

What stage of the writing process are you in?

What difficulties are you facing at this stage?

At what point in time do you see yourself publishing?

Have you decided on self- or traditional publishing?

If undecided, what questions do you have about:

Self-publishing...

Traditional publishing...

Writing

MY WRITING ROUTINE | TIME PER DAY | WORD COUNT

Make a writing schedule, & keep on track! A visual representation of realistic goal setting is highly beneficial to accoplishing your writing plan.

Editing

FIRST ROUND: | SECOND ROUND: | THIRD ROUND:

FOURTH ROUND: | FIFTH ROUND: | SIXTH ROUND:

Keep track of your edits. In each round, you look for something different. Use your Path To Authorship guide for reference.

Website & Social Media

MY WEBSITE | MY SOCIAL MEDIA HANDLE |

When about halfway done writing your manuscript, you should begin looking into your marketing stragety, I recommend using your name along with "author" across all platforms. Example: authorelsakurt or elsakurtauthor (all one word for username, page or site name would be Author Elsa Kurt or Elsa Kurt, Author.

Publishing

SELF PUBLISH ON: | TRADITIONALLY PUBLISH BY:

How do you want to publish, and when? For self-publishing, give yourself a reasonable deadline. For seeking traditional publishing, set query goals.

25 Glossary of Common Terms

Anthology: A book that's a collection of articles or stories written by several people.

ARC: Pre-publication advance review copy or advance reader copy. Send this when looking for media/trade/literary reviews, reader reviews you wanted posted as soon as you officially publish the book, and blurbs from endorsers (see below).

Back matter: Material at the end of the book, including the author bio, a list of other books from the author, and enticements to join the author's mailing list.

Beta Reader: These are your (unpaid) pre-release readers. Pick a handful, hand out your MS & give them a deadline for when you'd like their critiques back.

Binding: How a printed book is assembled between the covers. A book's spine results from the binding process. Paperback books typically have a "perfect binding" but other binding options include saddle stitching and spiral coil.

Blurb: An endorsement or testimonial from an influencer. (Some people also refer to the book's description as a "blurb.") A blurb goes on the front and/or back cover, online sales pages, your website, and, when there are a lot of them, inside the book as part of the front matter (see below).

Book proposal: A detailed document that's used to secure a nonfiction book publisher. It has many sections, including an overview, audience description, table of contents, and sample chapters.

Callout: Boxed text used as a graphic element in a nonfiction book.

Character: The star (or stars of your 'show')

Conflict: Here's the problem. No really, here's where you decide what the problem (or challenge) is going to be for your characters/storyline. There must be a conflict for there to be a story.

Copyright: Protects original works of authorship so others can't profit from it without your permission. Learn more at copyright.gov.

First Person: Point of view, uses "I" and "My" and "me"

Foreword: An introduction to the book from an influencer. Not to be confused with "forward." When the author writes the foreword, it's called a preface. (See below.)

Front matter: Pages that precede the main part of the book, where the story begins — blurbs, copyright, title, dedication, foreword, preface, introduction, table of contents, etc.

Galley: The edited book in typeset form without a cover. Used for proofreading and final author review instead of a PDF file. Sometimes used for blurbs and trade/media/literary reviews.Introduction: Appears after the table of contents of a nonfiction book to explain special features, highlight the book's structure, and provide specifics that might help the reader get as much as possible from the book.

ISBN: International Standard Book Number, an identifier that's unique to your book. It's required for retail sales of printed and audiobooks unless the author is the retailer

Literary Agent: An individual/company that represents authors in seeking publishing.

Logline: A one-sentence book description.

Metadata: Book specifics such as title, author name, publication date, description, size, keywords, and so on. Think of it as search engine optimization — SEO — for books. It helps your book get found in online searches.

MS: manuscript

MSS: manuscripts

Omniscient: all-seeing, all knowing POV

Pantser: A writer who lets the story unfold freely & unplanned

Planner/Plotter: One who plans out their MS

Plot: The meat of what happens in your story. from set up (introduction) to conflict (see below) to resolution (the end).

Point of View (POV): Who's telling the story? First-person ("I") Third person (he/she) Limited (one character's perspective) or omniscient (all-knowing narration). Be consistent, whatever you choose. Oh, and don't use second person (you) for storytelling. It rarely, if ever, reads well.

Preface: The author's story behind the nonfiction book — why the author wrote it, etc. It appears in the front matter.

Print on demand/POD: A publishing method that allows a company to print a single book only when there's an order. Amazon CreateSpace is a POD publisher.

Proof copy: Sometimes referred to as a galley (see above), it's the edited manuscript that the proofreader uses.

Query: Sending (via email, form, snail mail) requests for representation (by literary agents) or submitting a MS for consideration to a publishing house. This requires specific instructions/guidelines to be followed.

Setting: This is where the story takes place & can be one or multiple locations and/or time periods.

Special market/special sales: Non-bookstore retail outlets and opportunities, such as health clubs, museums, and gift shops.

Street team: Volunteers who agree to help you share information about your book among their social networks and elsewhere in an organized manner under your direction. Responsibilities usually include writing and posting an honest review on retail sites that include Amazon, BN.com, and Goodreads.

Style: This is the sound of your story - how things are said. Is your MC a fast-talking, slick dude? Or a proper lady? Is it a rom-com with quick, witty banter or an epic sci-fi adventure with nerd-speak (I'm kidding, I'm kidding).

Theme: This is the why of your story. What's the reason for it? What do you want your readers to understand?

Third person: POV using "he," "she," "they"

Tone: What's the vibe of the story, emotionally? Upbeat? Humorous? Melancholy?

W.I.P.: this is your manuscript, aka Work In Progress

26 Final Words

It is my sincere hope that this guide has answered your questions and given you a clearer view of the writing, publishing, and promoting journey. While I know not every single aspect of the process has been addressed, this is what I consider the essentials. Should you have more questions, or simply want a more individualized assistance, I offer one on one mentoring sessions to help you navigate the process. Email me at authorelsakurt@gmail.com to set up your first consultation. If you'd like to know more about me, visit https://elsakurt.com or on Facebook If you're curious about my books, visit my Amazon Author Central page.

www.ingramcontent.com/pod-product-compliance
Lightning Source LLC
Chambersburg PA
CBHW042130100526
44587CB00026B/4238